America's Game
New York
Mets

CHRIS W. SEHNERT

ABDO & Daughters
PUBLISHING

Published by Abdo & Daughters, 4940 Viking Dr., Suite 622, Edina, MN 55435.

Cover photo: Allsport
Interior photos: Wide World Photo, pages 1, 5, 7, 9-14, 16-20, 23, 25, 27.

Edited by Paul Joseph

Library of Congress Cataloging–in–Publication Data

Sehnert, Chris W.
    New York Mets / Chris W. Sehnert
        p. cm. — (America's game)
    Includes index.
    Summary: Focuses on key players and events in the history of the New York Mets, from their formation in 1962 through their up and down seasons over the next thirty-plus years.
    ISBN 1-56239-665-X
    1. New York Mets (Baseball team)—History—Juvenile literature.
[1. New York Mets (Baseball team). 2. Baseball—History.]
I. Title. II. Series.
GV875.N45S45   1997
796.357'64'097471—dc20   96-8144
                                                            CIP
                                                            AC

Contents

New York Mets

The New York Mets professional baseball team is younger than most organizations in Major League Baseball. It plays in the city where baseball grew up. With a relatively short timeline, the Mets have produced some of the greatest ballplayers and most thrilling moments in the history of the game.

In the early 1960s, the "Amazin' Mets" began as a troop of lovable losers, led by the aging baseball legend Casey Stengel. By the end of the decade, Tom Seaver led a miraculous turnaround that brought New York the 1969 World Championship.

Seaver and the Mets returned to the World Series in 1973. The team soon reversed course, falling back to the basement of the National League (NL) by the end of its second decade.

Darryl Strawberry and Dwight Gooden powered an awesome New York lineup in the 1980s. After one of the most outstanding seasons on record, the 1986 Mets were back on top. They played the Boston Red Sox in what was truly a "Fall Classic." With the jaws of defeat clamping down, the Mets rallied to win their second World Championship.

Today, the New York Mets are attempting to revive the miracles of their past. They look for Jeff Kent, Carl Everett, and Jason Isringhausen to take their place in the long line of great New York ballplayers.

The Mets' Dwight Gooden concentrates before delivering a pitch against the Pittsburgh Pirates.

Stengel's Lovable Losers

The rich tradition of baseball in New York City was carried on by the Giants, Dodgers, and Yankees until 1958. That season, the Giant and Dodger organizations moved to California. New York City was left without an NL team for the first time in over 70 years.

In 1960, NL owners agreed to expand the league from 8 to 10 teams. The new organizations were to be located in Houston and New York City. The Houston Colt .45s (the original Astros) and New York Mets began play in 1962.

The Mets derived their name from the New York Metropolitans of the old American Association. The new Mets borrowed their team colors from another pair of historic New York ballclubs. They took the "Dodger Blue" and combined it with the orange lettering of the Giants. They also borrowed the Giants' former ballpark, the Polo Grounds, until Shea Stadium became their new home in 1964. The Mets' first manager was the man who led the New York Yankees to seven World Championships between 1949 and 1958.

Casey Stengel was 71 years old when he became the Mets' skipper in 1962. Stengel was already a baseball legend in New York. His career began as an outfielder for the Brooklyn Dodgers back in 1912. He also played three seasons with the Giants, before managing the Dodgers and Yankees.

Stengel was an unprecedented promoter of baseball. While playing for the Pittsburgh Pirates in 1918, Stengel caught a sparrow, and hid the bird beneath his cap. Fans at Brooklyn's Ebbets Field were booing the former Dodger unmercifully. When Stengel emerged from the dugout to face more of the same, he tipped his cap to the New York crowd as the sparrow flew off his head. From that day forward, Casey Stengel would remain a favorite in the hearts of New York's faithful fans.

But beneath his clown-like image was the mind of a master baseball strategist. The 1962 New York Mets, however, were beyond any help Casey could provide on the field.

The first regular-season game the Mets were to play was a rain-out in St. Louis. The next day, the Cardinals defeated New York 11-4. What followed was a season of record-setting futility.

Mets' Manager Casey Stengel says farewell to the Polo Grounds on September 18, 1963. The team moved to Shea Stadium the following season.

The Mets suffered through losing streaks of 11, 13, and 23 games in their inaugural season. They lost 120 of their 160 contests to finish in last place, 60.5 games out of first! Incredibly, the "Amazin' Mets" drew nearly as many fans as the New York Yankees, who were the 1962 American League (AL) Champions.

The Mets' roster was filled with former heroes of New York baseball. Gil Hodges, a member of Brooklyn's "Boys of Summer" in the 1950s, was the Mets' original first baseman. Roger Craig and Don Zimmer, both former Dodgers and future major league managers, also served under Stengel on baseball's worst team. In 1963, Hall-of-Famer Duke Snider joined the flock of Dodgers who had become Mets.

Richie Ashburn played most of his Hall-of-Fame career with the Philadelphia Phillies. He led the Mets with a .306 batting average in 1962. But the Mets were also saddled with the likes of Marv Throneberry. He once hit a two-run triple, only to be called out for failing to touch first base. When Stengel came out to argue the call, the umpire quickly informed Casey that Throneberry had also missed second base.

The Mets continued their losing ways for several seasons, while their fans continued to fill the ballpark. With their third straight last-place finish in 1964, the Mets surpassed the "Bronx Bombers" in attendance. Apparently, the Yankees fifth straight AL Pennant was no match for the lovable losers who played across town.

A broken hip forced Casey Stengel to retire midway through the 1965 season. Once again, the Mets finished in last place. In his first five seasons as the Yankee manager, Stengel brought home a record five straight World Championships. With the "Amazin' Mets," he managed four straight NL "cellar-dwellers." Win or lose, he made the ballpark a fun place to be. Casey Stengel was inducted into the Baseball Hall of Fame in 1966.

Tom Seaver winds up to pitch during the 1973 World Series against the Oakland Athletics.

Miraculous!

A common way of maligning the New York Mets in the early 1960s was to say, "Man will walk on the moon before the Mets win a championship." In this case, the slander turned out to be true, but not by much.

Wes Westrum became New York's manager when Casey Stengel retired. In 1966, Westrum guided the Mets out of the NL cellar for the first time. They finished second-to-last, just in front of the Chicago Cubs. The next year the Mets were back on the bottom, despite the efforts of their star pitcher and NL Rookie of the Year, Tom Seaver.

Gil Hodges replaced Westrum before the 1968 season. For the second straight year, the Mets brought up an outstanding rookie pitcher. Jerry Koosman finished second in the 1968 NL Rookie of the Year balloting. New York finished one game in front of the Houston Astros to avoid their sixth last-place finish in seven years.

The NL expanded again in 1969, bringing the Montreal Expos and San Diego Padres into the league. Divisional play was setup that season, and the New York Mets became members of the NL East. The season started like all the others, with the Mets quickly falling off the pace.

9

Mets' pitcher Jerry Koosman.

Suddenly, an 11-game winning streak in early June gave the Mets more wins than losses. Tom Seaver emerged as one of the league's top pitchers, and New York threatened the Chicago Cubs for the division lead.

Seaver and Koosman were joined on the Mets' pitching staff by rookie Gary Gentry, and a fireballing Texan named Nolan Ryan. A nine-game winning streak in July was culminated by Seaver's one-hit shutout over the Cubs. "Tom Terrific" was just heating up, and one week later the Mets were only three games out of first place.

Tommie Agee and Cleon Jones powered the Mets offense. The two had grown up together in Mobile, Alabama. Agee won the 1966 AL Rookie of the Year Award, playing for the Chicago White Sox. In 1968, he joined his childhood friend in New York's outfield.

On September 11, 1969, the *New York Times'* headline told the story, "METS IN FIRST PLACE!" Surging to the finish line, the Mets won 22 of their final 27 games, as the Cubs faded out of sight. New York took the very first NL East Division title by eight games over Chicago. The "Miracle Mets" were just getting started.

Tom Seaver's 25 wins led the league, and he was named the 1969 NL Cy Young Award winner. Cleon Jones' .340 batting average was the league's third highest. The Mets faced the Atlanta Braves in the first National League Championship Series (NLCS).

The Braves won the NL West Division on the strength of Hank Aaron's 44 home runs. "Hammerin' Hank" crushed homers in all three games of the 1969 NLCS. Each time he put the Braves in front, the Mets managed to come back and win. In Game 3, Aaron hit a two-run homer in the third inning. Out of New York's bullpen came Nolan Ryan.

The 22 year-old kid, with the 100-m.p.h. fastball, had yet to establish himself as a premier strikeout artist. Ryan sent seven Braves down swinging in seven innings. His winning performance completed New York's three-game sweep to give the Mets their first NL Pennant!

Mets' fastball artist Nolan Ryan.

The 1969 World Series featured the powerful Baltimore Orioles versus the miraculous Mets. In Game 1, the Orioles beat Tom Seaver. Jerry Koosman kept Baltimore hitless through six innings of Game 2, as New York evened the Series at one game apiece.

In Game 3, Gentry and Ryan combined to shutout Baltimore, and Tommie Agee did the rest. Agee homered in the first inning, and followed it up with two outstanding run-saving catches in center field. Seaver's 10-inning gem in Game 4 left the Mets one win from glory.

Koosman finished off the Orioles with his second win of the Series, and the New York Mets were the 1969 World Champions. The Mets proved to everyone that miracles can happen.

Nolan Ryan is congratulated by teammates after striking out Baltimore Oriole Paul Blair to end the third World Series game in favor of the Mets, 5-0. From left: Jerry Grote, Wayne Garrett, Tom Seaver, Nolan Ryan, Jerry Koosman, Bud Harrelson, and trainer Gus Mauch.

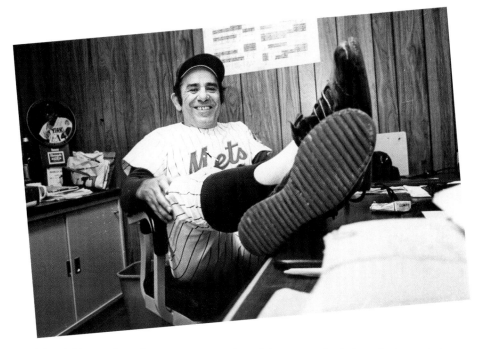

Yogi Berra is a happy man after his team led the Oakland A's three games to two during the 1973 World Series.

"It Ain't Over 'Til It's Over"

The Mets followed their 1969 "Miracle" season with three straight third-place finishes. Two days before his 48th birthday, Gil Hodges died of a heart attack. Another New York baseball legend, Yogi Berra, replaced Hodges as manager of the Mets in 1972.

Berra played on more World Championship teams (10) than any other person in major league history. He owes a great deal of his success to Casey Stengel, who made him the Yankees' everyday catcher in 1949.

The Mets continued to receive league-leading pitching in the early 1970s. Tom Seaver led the NL in earned run average (ERA) and strikeouts three times in the first four years of the decade. Nolan Ryan was traded to the California Angels in 1972. "The Ryan Express" went on to lead the AL in strikeouts seven times in the next eight years.

A tight race for the 1973 NL East Division caused Yogi Berra to utter his most prophetic words. The Mets had fallen to last place in late August, when Yogi told his team, "It ain't over 'til it's over." And he was right. The Mets began to move up from the cellar.

New York's ace relief pitcher was Tug McGraw. McGraw's patented screwball pitch had a lot to do with New York's turnaround. Many of his 25 saves that season came during the crucial September

Tug McGraw pitching against the Oakland A's during Game 7 of the 1973 World Series.

stretch drive. Seaver, meanwhile, picked up his second Cy Young Award, and once again the Mets made believers out of everyone.

New York won its second NL East title, despite having the weakest offense in the division. They faced Cincinnati's "Big Red Machine" in the 1973 NLCS. The Reds had the best record in baseball that season, and were heavily favored to dismantle the light-hitting Mets.

Tom Seaver did all he could to hold off the mighty Reds in Game 1. His RBI double gave the Mets a 1-0 lead, which he held intact through the first seven innings. Home runs by Johnny Bench and Pete Rose ruined a 13-strikeout performance by Seaver as Cincinnati grabbed the early series lead.

Rusty Staub provided all the offense the Mets would need in the next two games. He homered once in Game 2, and twice in Game 3, as New York jumped in front two games to one in the best-of-five series. Pete Rose hit his second game-winning homer of the NLCS in Game 4.

In the final game of the series, Seaver returned. Again he held the Reds to two runs. A very special pinch-hitter helped Seaver and the Mets hold on for victory.

Willie Mays played 21 seasons as a member of the Giants. The "Say Hey Kid" was the 1951 NL Rookie of the Year, back when the Giants played in New York City. In 1972, Willie Mays returned to New York to join the Mets. His RBI single put New York ahead to stay in Game 5 of the 1973 NLCS.

Tug McGraw recorded the final out, and the Mets were the NL Champions for the second time. The Mets faced the Oakland Athletics in the 1973 World Series. Willie Mays collected the last hit of his illustrious career in the 12th inning of Game 2. It produced another game-winning RBI for the Mets. The Athletics, however, recorded their second of three-straight World Championships in seven games.

New York never finished higher than third place in the NL East for the remainder of the decade. Yogi Berra managed his last game for the Mets in 1975. That season, Tom Seaver led the NL in wins, with 22, for the second time. Seaver was traded to the Cincinnati Reds in 1977.

Seaver returned to the Mets in 1983. The next year, he moved to the AL, where he pitched the final three seasons of his career. With 311 wins and a 2.86 lifetime ERA, Tom Seaver had the necessary credentials to join Willie Mays and Yogi Berra in the Baseball Hall of Fame.

Rusty Staub at bat against the Oakland A's during Game 7 of the 1973 World Series.

Dwight Gooden, right-handed ace for the Mets.

New Breed

The New York Mets ended the 1970s by finishing last in the NL East three straight times. In 1980, the team's new ownership hired Frank Cashen as general manager. Cashen had built the Baltimore Orioles into an AL powerhouse in the late 1960s. He soon set out to repeat the accomplishment in New York.

In a few short years, virtually the entire Mets lineup was changed. The overhaul included veteran players obtained through free agency or trades, mixed in with young talent. Davey Johnson was hired as manager in 1984 to bring the team together on the field.

Johnson was a star second baseman for the Orioles in the late 1960s. He made the final out of the 1969 World Series, when his fly ball to Cleon Jones completed New York's "Miracle" season. This time around, Johnson was expected to bring the Mets a championship.

Darryl Strawberry was brought up from the minor leagues in 1983. He was the NL Rookie of the Year that season, and an NL All-Star six times over the next eight seasons. In 1984, pitcher Dwight Gooden gave the Mets back-to-back award-winning rookies.

New York

Casey Stengel joined the Mets as manager in 1962 at age 71.

Tom Seaver was the 1967 NL Rookie of the Year.

In 1968, pitcher Jerry Koosman finished second in the NL Rookie of the Year balloting.

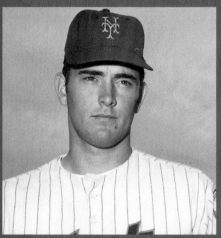

In Game 3 of the 1969 World Series, 22-year-old pitcher Nolan Ryan helped shutout the Baltimore Orioles.

Mets

Darryl Strawberry won the 1983 NL Rookie of the Year Award.

Dwight Gooden was only 19 years old when he won the 1984 NL Rookie of the Year Award.

Keith Hernandez, Gold Glove Award-winning first baseman, was a key part of the 1986 World Championship team.

Third baseman Bobby Bonilla joined the Mets in 1992 after four straight All-Star appearances for the Pittsburgh Pirates.

"Doc" Gooden was 19 years old when he won the Rookie of the Year Award, making him the youngest player ever to receive the award. He became the first teenager to lead Major League Baseball in strikeouts with 276, setting the all-time record for a rookie. Gooden was also the youngest player to appear in an All-Star game.

Joining Gooden and Strawberry in the Mets new lineup were Keith Hernandez and Gary Carter. Both players were renowned for their defensive abilities. Hernandez came from the St. Louis Cardinals, where he began his 11-year streak as the NL's Gold Glove first baseman. Carter won the Gold Glove for catchers three straight times with the Montreal Expos. Together, they provided veteran leadership for a team suddenly rising.

In 1985, Dwight Gooden became the youngest player ever to win the Cy Young Award. Doc performed a pitching Triple Crown, leading the NL in wins (24), strikeouts (268), and ERA (1.53). New York finished with its best record since their 1969 World Championship season. The Cardinals finished three games ahead of the Mets in the NL East, however.

The 1986 New York Mets won more games (108) than any team in the history of the franchise. They blew away the competition, taking their third division title by 21.5 games over the Philadelphia Phillies. As a team, the Mets combined the league's top batting average (.263) with the league's lowest ERA (3.11). This New York team was no lovable loser performing miracles. It was a new breed of hard-nosed champions.

Facing page: Darryl Strawberry lays down his bat as he watches his winning home run in a game against the Montreal Expos.

Exemplary of the Mets' style was Lenny Dykstra. In his second season, "Nails" had already gained a reputation for banging the center field fence with his body as well as with the line drives that came off his bat. The pesky New York leadoff-man played a key role in the postseason.

The 1986 NLCS was a six-game struggle between the New York Mets and the Houston Astros. Leading Houston's pitching staff were the 1986 NL Cy Young Award winner Mike Scott, and 20-year veteran Nolan Ryan. Baseball's all-time strikeout leader had returned to the NL in 1980. He faced his former team in a battle for the NL Pennant.

Mike Scott outdueled Dwight Gooden (1-0) in the series opener, as the Astros took Game 1. In Game 2, the Mets jumped on Nolan Ryan, as New York's Bob Ojeda went the distance to even the series. Dykstra's ninth-inning homer in Game 3 provided the margin for the Mets' second victory. Scott picked up his second win of the series with a three-hitter in Game 4.

Nolan Ryan returned in Game 5, striking out 12 and allowing the Mets just 2 hits through 9 innings. One of the hits was a Darryl Strawberry homer, which tied the score 1-1. Gary Carter's 12th-inning single drove in the winning run for the Mets.

With New York leading the series three games to two, the Mets needed a victory in Game 6 to avoid facing the red-hot Mike Scott for a third time. After 16 innings, in the longest postseason game in major league history, Mets' reliever Jesse Orosco struck out the last Astro, leaving the winning run stranded on base. The New York Mets had their third NL Pennant.

Facing page: Keith Hernandez smacks one over the right field fence for a home run against the Philadelphia Phillies.

Miracle Or Curse?

The 1986 World Series was every bit as unforgettable as the NLCS. The Boston Red Sox, looking to win their first World Championship since trading Babe Ruth in 1919, came one strike away. The Mets had one more miracle up their sleeve.

The Red Sox won the first two games of the Series at New York's Shea Stadium. The Mets were already in a position from which no team had ever come back to win. Lenny Dykstra led off Game 3 with a home run at Fenway Park, and New York posted its first victory, 7-1. Dykstra slammed another homer in Game 4, and Gary Carter added two shots of his own as the Mets evened the Series.

Game 5 belonged to Boston as the Red Sox jumped on Doc Gooden for nine hits in the first four innings. The Series moved back to Shea Stadium for Game 6. Pitching for Boston was the 1986 AL Cy Young Award winner, Roger Clemens. New York was facing elimination.

The Mets and Red Sox battled to a 3-3 tie through nine innings. Boston scored two runs in the top of the tenth, and were just three outs away from a championship. Red Sox relief pitcher Calvin Schiraldi got the first two outs on fly balls. New York hung on, with singles by Gary Carter and Kevin Mitchell. Ray Knight fell behind with no balls and two strikes, bringing Boston to within one strike of the title. Knight singled to center, scoring Carter, moving Mitchell to third, and driving Schiraldi from the game.

Mookie Wilson faced Bob Stanley in one of the most memorable at-bats in World Series history. The New York crowd chanted "MOOOOO-kie" as their popular left fielder stepped to the plate. Stanley got ahead of Wilson with two strikes, bringing the Red Sox to within one strike of World Series glory for the second time.

Refusing to strike out, Mookie fouled off the next two pitches to stay alive. Stanley's seventh pitch to Wilson was wild. It scored Kevin Mitchell from third base to tie the score. After two more foul balls, Mookie hit a squibbing groundball down the first base line. Somehow, the ball rolled through the legs of Red Sox first baseman Bill Buckner. Ray Knight scored on the error, and the Mets had evened the Series at three games each.

Ray Knight and Darryl Strawberry homered in Game 7, and New York was victorious. For Boston, "Babe's Curse" had prevailed. The New York Mets were the 1986 World Champions!

Mookie Wilson attempts a diving catch in a game against the Cincinnati Reds.

Revival

The Mets won their fourth NL East Division title in 1988. They were strengthened by the addition of pitcher David Cone. Darryl Strawberry led the NL in home runs with 39, and finished second in the NL MVP balloting. New York was defeated in the 1988 NLCS by the Los Angeles Dodgers.

Team captains Gary Carter and Keith Hernandez were released after the 1989 season. Manager Davey Johnson was replaced by Bud Harrelson in 1990. Strawberry became a Los Angeles Dodger in 1991. Howard Johnson provided a glimmer of hope in New York that season, leading the NL in home runs with 38, and RBIs with 117. The Mets, however, were unquestionably in full decline.

In 1992, Mets' pitcher Anthony Young began a personal losing streak that covered two seasons. When he finally defeated the Florida Marlins in July 1993, his 27 consecutive losses had set a new major league record. His hard work and positive attitude throughout the string of futility made him one more lovable loser in Mets' history.

Facing page: Third baseman Bobby Bonilla goes airborne trying to throw out a batter.

New York's lineup became a revolving door for some of the league's top talent in the early 1990s. Former Cy Young Award winners Frank Viola and Brett Saberhagen failed to produce similar results in a Mets' uniform. Bobby Bonilla made four straight All-Star appearances for the Pittsburgh Pirates before joining New York in 1992. After three disappointing seasons with his hometown Mets, Bonilla was traded to the Baltimore Orioles.

New York climbed out of the NL East's cellar in 1995. A corps of young pitchers, including Jason Isringhausen, Bill Pulsipher, and Paul Wilson, were expected to lead New York into the future. The new manager, Dallas Green, would try to conduct the revival. New York Mets' fans understand, in baseball, all things are possible.

Glossary

All-Star: A player who is voted by fans as the best player at one position in a given year.

American League (AL): An association of baseball teams formed in 1900 which make up one-half of the major leagues.

American League Championship Series (ALCS): A best-of-seven-game playoff with the winner going to the World Series to face the National League Champions.

Batting Average: A baseball statistic calculated by dividing a batter's hits by the number of times at bat.

Earned Run Average (ERA): A baseball statistic which calculates the average number of runs a pitcher gives up per nine innings of work.

Fielding Average: A baseball statistic which calculates a fielder's success rate based on the number of chances the player has to record an out.

Hall of Fame: A memorial for the greatest baseball players of all time located in Cooperstown, New York.

Home Run (HR): A play in baseball where a batter hits the ball over the outfield fence scoring everyone on base as well as the batter.

Major Leagues: The highest ranking associations of professional baseball teams in the world, currently consisting of the American and National Baseball Leagues.

Minor Leagues: A system of professional baseball leagues at levels below Major League Baseball.

National League (NL): An association of baseball teams formed in 1876 which make up one-half of the major leagues.

National League Championship Series (NLCS): A best-of-seven-game playoff with the winner going to the World Series to face the American League Champions.

Pennant: A flag which symbolizes the championship of a professional baseball league.

Pitcher: The player on a baseball team who throws the ball for the batter to hit. The pitcher stands on a mound and pitches the ball toward the strike zone area above the plate.

Plate: The place on a baseball field where a player stands to bat. It is used to determine the width of the strike zone. Forming the point of the diamond-shaped field, it is the final goal a base runner must reach to score a run.

RBI: A baseball statistic standing for *runs batted in.* Players receive an RBI for each run that scores on their hits.

Rookie: A first-year player, especially in a professional sport.

Slugging Percentage: A statistic which points out a player's ability to hit for extra bases by taking the number of total bases hit and dividing it by the number of at bats.

Stolen Base: A play in baseball when a base runner advances to the next base while the pitcher is delivering his pitch.

Strikeout: A play in baseball when a batter is called out for failing to put the ball in play after the pitcher has delivered three strikes.

Triple Crown: A rare accomplishment when a single player finishes a season leading their league in batting average, home runs, and RBIs. A pitcher can win a Triple Crown by leading the league in wins, ERA, and strikeouts.

Walk: A play in baseball when a batter receives four pitches out of the strike zone and is allowed to go to first base.

World Series: The championship of Major League Baseball played since 1903 between the pennant winners from the American and National Leagues.

Index